Praise for E

Ralph Earle's poetry is like spring, companionable, con here with these poems, safe enough to leave your front door open and to let them come into your life, mind, and heart. They have so much to give: insight, humor, surprise, and delight. They are not without sadness, because after all that's *The Way the Rain Works*, to borrow from Earle's earlier chapbook, some of whose poems find a welcome second home here, because all of our experiences are carefully voiced in these poems. Having spent lovely hours, awake not asleep, with these poems, I too can say "Let Us All Be Happy" and mean it, not just for myself, not just for my companions on a train, but for everyone.

—Paul Jones, author of *Something Wonderful*

In this luminous collection, Ralph Earle contemplates his life and ours, as we "cross the darkness on a bridge of reed / between the ruin and the radiance." In poems that dazzle with surprising metaphors, precise language and close observations of nature, Earle relates his journey as son, brother, husband, father, grandfather and seeker of the Absolute. "Life writes its stories on us," he says, and narrates his with quiet lyricism. Early in his marriage, "days carried us weightless / as paper lanterns in the trees." Later his wife's mental illness worsens: "wheeling out of the blue sky / of what we expected…." His gaze is clear and compassionate. He considers violence, oppression and injustice, the climate calamity, and waits for America "to walk off a cliff / clutching its…red-white-and-blue / umbrella." Even so, these shimmering poems invite us to regard every moment as "a lake / brimming with light."

—Janis Harrington, author of *How to Cut a Woman in Half, Waiting for the Hurricane*

These poems are meditations composed of spiritual insights that emerge from Ralph Earle's close observation of everyday events, the voices of those who've come before, and encounters with the strange and inexplicable nature of the world. Each poem is voiced with an innocent wisdom and subtle humor constructed from his personal fears, social-political perspectives, and reflections on the natural world.

His section, "Cold Days in Eden," reveals a deeply compassionate and intense exploration of the challenges and rewards of family life while "Enter the Weather" is an honest self-exploration. He writes: "The weather of our lives / begins to turn." It is in this turning that one finds solace and pain, regret and pleasure.

These poems are insightful, private and honest in their perspectives. As he writes in the last poem in the collection: "as we slowly take our leave of this world / so random and so transient, let us all be happy." Earle's passionate skill, quiet and intense, is an empathetic reach into the very heart of living.

—Chapman Hood Frazier, author of *The Lost Books of the Bestiary*

Also by this Author:

> *Enterprise Computing with Objects: From Client/Server to the Internet* (Reading, MA: Addison-Wesley, 1998), with Yen-Ping Shan.

> *The Way the Rain Works* (Greensboro, NC: Sable Books, 2015).

Everything You Love Is New

Poems

Ralph Earle

REDHAWK
PUBLICATIONS

ISBN: 978-1-959346-36-4 (Paperback)

Library of Congress Control Number: 2024930346

Any references to historical events, real people, or real places are used fictitiously. Names, characters, and places are products of the author's imagination.

Front cover image by Ethan Earle.
Book design by Robert T Canipe.

Printed in the United States of America.

First printing edition 2024.

Redhawk Publications
The Catawba Valley Community College Press
2550 Hwy 70 SE
Hickory NC 28602

For Ethan, Luke,
Marcel, and Anne

There are a hundred thousand species of love, separately invented, each more ingenious than the last.
~ Richard Powers (b. 1957)

Love is the bridge between you and everything.
~ Jelal ud-Din Rumi (1207 – 1273)

Contents

Bring Me Back the Change

What Becomes of the Strawberries

my mother says she will be gone a moment
and bring me strawberries
a moment means away and back

strawberries sweeping over me
like sun chasing the clouds

strawberries coming to the car for me

grey back seat, door handle, blue-white sky
the stalk of the lock means away and back

clouds cross strawberries
grey becomes sky

no back only away
up down alone
down i lie

face prickles
green tree above makes me ripple

lock pops door swings car starts
driving home

where are my strawberries?

                                              oh, there weren't any

the way she talks when dinner burns

A Man Like You Deserves French Fries

Behind a counter where flawless
cabinets flick out straws,
three machine tenders in green
and white await my word. I call
to one, a young girl near a tall
thing like an injection mold,
offer the change in my pocket
for something thick and cold
with chocolate
she can dump in a cup.
Her smile slides its fingers up my thighs.
She says *A man like you deserves French fries.*

Beirut Holiday Inn, 67 A.D.

You find yourself in the lounge
drinking a Brandy Alexander
trying to stay calm. At your elbow
a kid with red hair stares at his fingers,
a Swiss flag sewed to his army jacket back.

He is into prophecies, like you,
reads a lot of Jesus, likes Habakkuk
and Jonah too. When he says something sharp
about the end of Jack the Baptist, you relax
and with a few fast facts show
that Jeremiah foresaw this catastrophe
and though Caligula was sharp
as a Philistine's eyetooth,
it was noble Augustus
really knew the angles.

The kid's attention drifts
to the TV hanging in darkness:
bread and circuses
live
from the Colosseum.

When I Hitchhiked to Big Sur

Ginger and Janet stopped
in their cluttered Oldsmobile
as evening came on.

Twenty miles down the coast
under spring rainclouds
we laid our sleeping bags
on a deserted beach
and told each other stories.

A wild-haired stranger
stumbled into our circle
clutching a bayonet
in a shaky hand and shouting
about the flashback he was in.

Ginger and Janet lay
quiet as sand dunes.

Even as I told myself
to hunker down too,
something inside
sat up a most sociable version of me
and asked if he'd seen the sunset.

As I chatted cheerily, the weird light
drained from his eyes and he left.

I bathed in the women's admiration.

Later in the quiet drizzle
Janet told me she couldn't—
that her boyfriend would kill her—
but she wished she could.

We lay against each other's backs
in our separate sleeping bags
and the dark cliffs rose above us.

Hills and Headlands

These are the same hills and headlands,
eucalyptus on the ridge,
the far beaches that make my heart cry.

Years ago, driving these hairpin turns,
I listened to my teacher
telling me about the Absolute.

Now the ego seeks in vain
to find its way back along
this coastal highway of revelation.

All signs point to my Beloved's
limitless imagination, the lower self
a mirror to the radiance.

Oh I wish I had given myself
to my Beloved in those early
twilights when I drove

down the mountain to the beach,
fog rising off the ocean.

The School of the Patient Heart

In smoky afternoon light
surrounded by their students
two bearded patriarchs
sit facing on a Persian carpet.

After a long silence, the elder
insists we must align ourselves
with the world we have inherited,
complex beyond imagining,
its operating system our soul,
our destiny in its circuits.

The younger, almost maternal one
asks us rather to consider
a ream of printer paper,
cheap and easily available.
We are blank sheets, he says
Life writes its stories on us,
we twist in the dark
machinery. The ink dries.

We discover ourselves
wherever the light suffices.

Nor Do They Talk

trees I cannot be without
nor do they talk

unlike poetry unlike
television but

an outpouring
a concentric emotion

as if the living wood
expanding year by

year to the horizon
all we know the

commonplace the lakeshore
encompasses us

growth rings
everywhere overlapping

Sometimes I Burn My Bridges

I cross and return, I do everything
to get out of myself, go deep
in the woods across creeks
on bridges two boards wide.
Sometimes I watch the stream
flow far away down the ravine

and sometimes I don't. I pray
the waters of change will unbind me
as I cross from one steep creekside
of trust to another. I take paths,
untangle thoughts, my choices blossom
and pass. The water carries their ashes.

This path is a thread I can barely see,
a highway many have walked, hearing
the thousand-voice river
against the shoals. Trees living and dead
line the banks. I cross a span the dusty
color of sycamore. Loose boards rattle.

Behind me is a life once held as worthy:
parking lot, families in picnic shelters,
young couple in the trees, trash cans
and tables. When I reach the wild side
I am nobody, I disappear with my fears
and imperfections. Only the river remains.

Ruin and Radiance

If the rain that is forever falling
would only wash us clean

what we hear of your voice
would enfold us in its resonance.

Grant us the words to bear
your light in this world of shadow,

words that translate the ineffable
into roots, leaves, shared fruit.

We cross the dark on a bridge of reed
between the ruin and the radiance.

The Cormorants Arrive

Like a gang of legislators
    dressed in grey
        from somewhere

outside of town,
    the cormorants loiter
        on the lake's little float

strutting a step or two,
    dropping
        into the water

for a fish.
    They represent
        some constituency

I don't recognize,
    shuffling around
        their little island.

They disturb me,
    they embody my fear
        of narrow minds,

of self-assured
    self-inflated strangers,
        fear of my own silence.

Still, when I approach
    they dwindle
        into a smattering

of awkward fishing birds,
    all angle and tackle, waiting
        their moment of excitement,

the shadow of small prey
    out of reach
        in the darkening water.

Any Snake Bears Watching

9 November 2016

Autumn is hot, the leaves dry and drop
into the stream. Against each rising rock,
a mob backs up. The stream is dark.

Sun flashes on ripples, then vanishes.
A heron watches from a dead branch.
On a random rock, scraps of a note

burned for some reason: charred border,
a few blue lines on white.
I cannot think about the vote last night.

Once, in this spot, I saw a brown and tan
snake swimming toward my dangling foot.
Copperhead or water snake?

Any snake bears watching.
From upstream above the trees
come explosions, like a celebration

as rocks are blasted in the nearby quarry
for trucks to haul away. Raindrops
spatter the water like bullets into bull's eyes.

The heron has not moved. The stream caresses
the tumbled stone, the way my fingers flowed
over your face before daylight, as we lay sleepless.

Bring Me Back the Change

Since Trayvon died I haven't felt so good.
He was too much like my son
in his sullen hoodie, restless
as any teen, wanting something
at the convenience store.

The difference is the privilege
that color carries, though
with hoodies pulled low enough,
one young man is like another.

Luke's best friend Terrence
played football at Ole Miss. As a boy
he would go with us to games
and at the party in the paintball park
he wore goggles and carried a gun
with his white classmates.

Luke would walk to Terrence's
even at night, quiet, trying
to outmaneuver the dark. He couldn't
sit still, he wanted to move,
he wanted to go to the store.
I would give him a five and tell him
bring me back the change.

One cloudy night last year
a black SUV followed me home,
and all I could think to do
was step forward to meet
the huge dark man who emerged.

It was only when he reached an arm
to hug me, like any young person
with a family friend, that I recognized
him, a man who had been a child.

There is no firearm
in this tale of what I fear and love.

Another Video

Tamir Rice, 2002 – 2014

He is a large child but if he were a man,
he would be small. The video shows him
playing by himself in a park under trees.
No sound. No one around.

He walks up and down with a toy weapon,
pointing, then pointing again, as I did
at his age, as my sons did in the backyard
and at the paintball park. The child sits on a bench.

Ten minutes pass. He begins to walk, toy weapon
put away, as if toward home. A squad car
pulls up. Two police jump out. The child falls.
It is so efficient. Someone sick with fear
must have called for this, called for a take-out order.

City of Thorns

*Founded in 1991 as a temporary shelter
for Somalis, the Dadaab complex in Kenya
now houses nearly half a million refugees.*
-Ben Rawlence,* City of Thorns*

The UN-issued tents rip apart
in less than a year, and so they weave
houses out of thornbushes, covered with plastic
on lanes arranged in a grid in a big camp
near the border in Kenya. Half a million
people live here, and when it rains
the mud is too deep to wade through, but you do
anyway, and the government does not allow
permanent structures.

If you want luxuries like tea and salt
you must trade away your Food Aid.
The reporter got to know the young people, they
told him this. They feel their lives have not begun.
The top ten boys and girls earn scholarships
at international universities. Refugee Resettlement
can manage 5,000 families and for those lucky few
the wait time is years.

The thin young people say you can trade
a week or more of rations for a cell phone.
Everyone has a cell phone, it's how they connect
with Minneapolis and Mogadishu, and across
the cake-mud ruts of the camp. They post photos
to Facebook and write fantasies in Somali about
going to Disneyland, about starring for a world-class
football team, riding to an implausible senior prom
on the shoulders of an elephant.

Bisous

a hard rain falling
an inconvenient truth
i am waiting for America
to walk off a cliff
clutching its   red-white-and-blue
umbrella
living with dignity
takes a conviction
lacked by all but the worst

a two-step   too easy
to be fooled   too easy to eat
outrage and despair   a strong current
pulls us toward morning
we wake up and witness

bisous-bisous-bisous say the birds

Green Patchwork of Morning

You wake up
and have your little
dialog with death
then you
wonder why your glasses
are on the floor.

Your mind
is a conveyer belt
bringing you
snatches of dreams
to assemble,

already flapping apart
in the winds of day:

a sad man
and woman
natter for attention,
prayer flags, the briefest
of smiles,

and down
the green
patchwork
of morning,
the only one you
loved, walking
into light.

Garth Brooks Plays Walmart

This best engine of commerce,
its very name like nothing
the language has produced before,
meaning something between gathering
and exchange, in aisles in narrow lanes
as far beyond this day's redemption
as half-remembered sound bites on the intercom.

This building's soul a dusty empty corridor
where loading dock attendants shoulder
bargains of every hue, as we shoppers scurry
among racks of clothing, as we hunt for our batteries,
our toiletries, our cheap decorative doormats

and Garth Brooks, they say, is in electronics,
in every electronics department
in every Walmart in the world,
playing a catchy glittery number for everyone
who shops at Walmart or works at Walmart
or drops into Walmart to experience Garth Brooks
singing the body electric on a sound stage
in Los Angeles while this best consumer edifice
picks up his TV feed.
                              Is this healthy?
A dull man greets me with a smile,
the doorkeeper. I float in fluorescence,
my skin pasty, the dreams and despair
of my fellow shoppers lapping at me
like the mingled waters of Discourse,
Recreation, and The Purse.

I have been dazzled, been reduced
to fingering off-brand golf balls
as I stand in the register line
and the terrible God of the Universe
that is here and then gone
waits at the final check-out.

The Small Kitchen Appliances Aisle

By the time I catch sight of Celeste,
I have lost track of what store I am in.
I came here for a vegetable brush, and
have been tossing every good deal
I might someday need into a shopping cart
whose wheels point in different directions.

Celeste trembles, surprised to see me
in such a place. She isn't sure
what she is looking for, just wandering.
She tells me I can find the vegetable brushes
on the small kitchen appliances aisle.

I try to persuade her to come with me
to the next meditation group, knowing
sometimes riding with me works for her,
and sometimes not. She recedes
down another aisle while I succeed
in spotting, like a rare bird, my brush.

I think I'll check out now. I think
I'll put my purchases in the trunk.
I'll yield to pedestrians, persuade myself
to re-park, return for that extra ream of paper,
low-fat cereal, overlooked cleanser,
one more word with Celeste.

Corporate American Waterfowl

They glower in the spring
from the designated smoking area,
walkway littered with their leavings.
A gander barks at a passing Lexus.
His partner, nesting nearby, hisses,
eyes two black beads, beak so wide
I can see down her black throat.

Near the erosion control pond in May
two adults stand sentry as goslings
the color of bank-side weeds nibble
the lawn's edge, strung between
the twin certainties of their parents.

In midsummer, the fledglings have grown
identical to their elders. I know them only
by the space they occupy, separate
but leaning toward one another,
edging toward the employee entrance.

My Life as an Orangutan

I hang, eating a banana,
from the branches my ceiling has sprouted
wondering about other orangutans—
though we are solitary creatures—
admiring our orange hair,
digging insects with our sticks.

In the Borneo jungle, we climb down
and walk the way people did
long ago when they first started out.

On a river dock we lather ourselves
with soap left behind by people,
pouring their basins of river water
over our bodies. Our hands
are their hands, our solemn lips theirs,
our eyes shining with wonder.

All around us, trees are falling.
Like people, we don't understand,
like them we hang around
eating bananas,
slathering ourselves with soap.

Early Morning Light

a wren snatches breakfast
out of the sycamore bark

the tussock moth caterpillar
dances on an invisible thread

ants in a line on the railing
always somewhere to go

other creatures so motionless
they might be dust motes

verbena flowers open
at the speed of day

birds vanish when my head nods
I watch leaves flutter

a small insect crosses the page
I breathe it to the ground

haiku written over days over weeks
all the same voice all singing

Cold Days in Eden

How We Lost the Beehives

Mr. Capuano, our apple man,
arched his eyebrow, gave me a smile,
and carried off our baskets in his truck.

We liked him, but in the spring
when the white blossoms came again
we had a new apple man named Ruta.

Capuano didn't have the right
to sell the lease said my mother
with a tight shake of her head.

One Saturday afternoon
when we returned from a swim,
cars and trucks were parked

all along the apple road.
Men in soiled rumpled shirts
stood in the orchard around tables

that had appeared from nowhere
heavy with food, and women
in dresses with polka dots.

We were witnessing a miracle:
red wine in glasses, kisses, laughter,
loud jokes, trees heavy with fruit.

My father called Ruta from the crowd
and had a quiet word. Ruta grimaced
and my father turned toward the house.

Every spring brought fewer blossoms
as the white-painted beehives faded
and grew empty. One spring they were gone

and my father taught us to play baseball
among the apple trees and poison ivy.

Second-Best Stooge

Three old red oaks overhung the lawn.
In football weather, Walter quarterbacked
and I ran pass patterns down and out
versus Freddy and the oaks. Walter
whispered the plays to me in advance.

We were the Three Stooges of Nod Hill Road.
In the spring, Walter tossed tricky pitches
for me to tag out Freddy between tree-bases.
When Freddy had a fit, Walter kept him in line
like Moe the Head Stooge did, with his knuckles.

I wanted to be funny and well-behaved
so Walter made me Larry, the quiet Stooge
with frizzy hair. I leaned into an oak
and delivered my punchlines to its bark.

Betty and Freddy Watch the Wrestling

On the black-and-white TV in her room,
Betty watched the local wrestling,
bad white boys acting proud
after all the little white boys fell asleep

except Freddy, who would steal
into her room where together
they'd watch Bruno Sammartino
pound on Haystack Calhoun.
They liked each other's company.

My mother talked about wrestling
the way she talked about
the big black headlines in the *Daily News*
that were bad for us but not for Betty,
a fact that Mother couldn't explain.

Weekends, when Betty took a taxi
back to Norwalk, we were under orders
to stay away from her room.
If Freddy turned up with a *Daily News*,
Mother buried it in the pile by the washer
where it waited for the Boy Scout paper drive.

Betty Helps Out

We didn't talk to her much.
By day, she stood in the kitchen
ironing in an old white uniform
or leaning back on the vinyl stepstool.
Evenings, she watched TV
in her bedroom far in the back.

Heavy and diabetic, she harbored
insulin syringes in the fridge,
which Mother warned us not to touch.

Mother never called Betty a maid.
She said *Betty helps us out.*

It was hard to read the expression
behind Betty's thick glasses.
In the light of memory
it comes to me as forbearance.

My father paid for the funeral
none of us attended.

Fallout Shelter

I don't care what it takes, we need one, said my
father. My mother asked what good it would do,
and I heard him try to get around something in her
voice, like a sailboat beating into the wind.

Below a bank of yellow forsythia, the garbage
cans occupied a half-rotten skid of wood in what
we called the Laundry Yard. Nobody saw me walk
out there with a shovel.

After an hour of attacking the gravely dirt, I
decided to build my fallout shelter above ground
instead. In the shed I found wood and nails, and
by dinner the wall reached to my armpits. My
father was at a meeting for Civil Defense.

The next day, my poem about a jigsaw puzzle won
first prize in the middle school poetry contest. The
puzzle was a world map that wouldn't go together
right.

We practiced huddling under our desks on the
gritty grey tile floor. It would have been fun if
boys and girls got to huddle together, but Miss
McMahon didn't seem to think so.

Or maybe she did, and it wasn't supposed to be
fun. We were shown photos of explosions, but
never in Japan. Today's bombs were a hundred
times bigger. *Duck and cover* didn't make sense, it
was just something we did.

When I came home, my fallout shelter was flat
on the ground with the garbage cans on top. My
mother beamed at me for surprising her with such
a useful platform. No point explaining. I was glad
she liked it.

Past the Edge of Eden

The pine thicket engulfs me, trees in thick rows.
Across my arm a branch draws a bead of blood.
With my every step, my forehead is nettled.
My breath is cut. I can't call it fun

like with friendlier trees closer to home,
piling green acorns into pyramids,
carving my initials in beech bark,
climbing the little magnolia in spring.

If I keep pushing through, I will reach
the marshy brook below the rock dam,
down with the copperheads and fallen logs,
down where skunk cabbage grows.

The First Girl I Kissed

We met in a dark bar drinking Grasshoppers
or was it Brandy Alexanders, bound for Europe
on the S.S. Nieuw Amsterdam. She said she
wanted me, but I wasn't sure. Your mother
kisses you. Someday, your wife does.

A few nights later, I was sitting in the bow
trying to make time with her older friend.
During the day, tired of pretending to be
eighteen, we commandeered a game room nook
where the jukebox moaned "Be My Baby."

Everyone was on vacation. One night
I climbed halfway up the radar mast
to catch a view of the moonlight
stippling the fickle ocean.

The Huge House among Trees

How strange to wish not to be part of
the party in the huge house among trees
where my cousin watches from her bearskin
as her boys from the city play pool.

How strange to wish not to take note of
the bleat of the stereo, breeze off the lake,
click of the white cue ball
against the black eight.

What will it take to walk out
on the green-trimmed antiques,
on my aunt growing ill
behind her grim drapes?

What will it take to steer into dark,
to walk out on the house
in its ragged horizon of trees?

We Lived on the Edge of Calamity

You demanded groceries after midnight,
a second desk, a dog, a piano.
Our roommates—a high-strung postman

and my one-time closest friend—
kicked us out. We both moved
back with our parents.

I drove too fast and wrecked the car.
Over the hospital phone I said I was fine.
You said you would kill yourself.

Your words slurred: you said you were dying.
The names of the pills you took?
You ought to know and *You wouldn't care.*

Would a dried-up riverbed call the police?
Would a broken-hearted lover? On the third day
you rose again and needed me.

I took my mother's car and drove fast
two hundred miles downstate to cradle you.

Snow Falling Silently

In the dark lake of the sky,
nets of naked branches
fish for the invisible morning.

Some days the sun never rises.
If I wake I lie rigid,
rehearsing the solace of the night.

No matter how often I start
the story differently, it ends
the same: the wind blows,

night grows old.
Snow falls in the silence.

First Light

You must hope what you notice
is different from the darkness,
something on the horizon,
a quickening, an assurance.

The crescent moon casts
a meager shadow.
A shooting star burns silent.

Constellations float
in the summer brightening—
the Swan, the Fishes.

They wash away
in the flood of dawn.
Every moment a lake
brimming with light.

West Virginia

Lightning bugs rise
     toward the thunderheads,
         Ann and I on a blanket

where the long grass ends,
     slow fireworks
         in the branches of our blood.

Days carry us weightless
     as paper lanterns in the trees.
         Thunder beyond the ridges.

Lightning bugs
     vanish like sparks
         on the wings of rain.

Emergency C-Section

As if we are traveling from mountains
into foothills toward an unknown destination,
the heart monitor's spiky horizon starts to smooth.

Ann and I have been breathing together
way too many hours for anything to go wrong.
Exhausted, she waits for the anesthetic.
I sit on a stool, and because we don't want mistakes
I reach for a bright pointed thing on the instrument tray.

Mr. Earle. The nurse's voice breaks the spell.
Her fingers touch mine. I ease my hand under my butt
to watch the incision made and the bloody baby raised,
thick purple cord around his neck like a noose
loosened quickly by the doctor: this child is innocent.

I hold him bundled in white. His tiny hands
fold under his chin as if still confined inside his mother.
When I lay my finger across his palm, his own fingers
close on it. His clear blue eyes greet me with wonder.

The Insulating Properties of Trees

Three white ducks waddle
among picnic tables and pine trees.
Nearby, a family celebrates, mother and girls
gathered, a vase with a red rose.

We expect the baby will start to scream.
Thanks to the insulating properties of trees
it will bother no one but us
and even that is beginning to blur.
He screams. Ann's face falls.
I take him against my shoulder
and follow the ducks toward the sound
of the rushing spillway.

Behind a tree
where we can't see his mother eating
we play this game: Sorry, Ann,
I put him down on the water a moment
like Moses, you know, and he just
floated away.

This is why
some people put babies up for sale
or hang their cradleboards in trees
all day long, in sycamores.

Frog in a Cardboard Box

When my first-born was little
we lived in a house that rattled
on a quiet side street in town.

After a spring rain, a rivulet ran down
between the trees to a marshy spot
back of the house, and a frog arrived.

We watched it in the early morning
and wondered where it would go
when the yard dried out. And so

we eased it into a cardboard box
and drove to the countryside
where a stream ran all year long.

The frog sat shining
on a slick rock, a jewel
received and given.

I woke up startled. I had fallen asleep
with the front open door, dreaming
of that time when my child and I

held something precious in a shoebox.
Moths fluttered around the porch light.
At my senses' edge, the velvet call of an owl.

Lee County Luncheonette, 1985

I'm angry with you
    renting your upstairs
        to them. No Coloreds

ever lived on
    our street.
        They're the first.

She wore clip-on earrings
    and carried her white handbag
        like a shield.

Ann and I were eating
    cheap soup downtown.
        I stared at my bowl,

my cracker packs,
    my afternoon shattered like
        red-rimmed chinaware

swept off the counter
    where shopkeepers hunched
        drinking their sweet tea.

Still Life with Shovel

All I want is to get the dead
      cat out of the street before
            Ann comes home

as if a tired man says something
      that breaks forever the bond
            of trust with his wife.

The cat moves so easily
      I want to pour the blood
            back into the small wounds.

Still Life with Chainsaw

In a dry ditch, thighs at road level,
I bring down young pines
that block our view.
A flock of birds appears:

first nothing, then black
specks flapping, then nothing.

Wheeling out of the blue sky
of what we expected,
my wife calls curses to herself.
They are here. They are gone.

If she had lost a hand
how would I resist
taking the chainsaw to my wrist

slender as a two-year pine,
leave the offending member
cradled by cut boughs
so she would know?

If I could, I would stitch
my hand to her wrist,
stitch it with pine needles,

mend the severed nerves. But who
would stand in the ditch? Who
with good hands release the sky?

Every Field of Paradise

In the moment between day's end
and settling into sleep,
things that have broken
vanish in a glowing sphere

around the brass Victorian
lamp my neighbor Ed gave us
as a wedding present, turned
on his lathe in the falling-down barn

behind our houses, where I
rambled through alfalfa and clover
in the pulse of crickets, under miles
of spilling stars encircling me

like the vision of paradise that day
I felt life leave my dog and saw him
run gladly through the endless green,
his spine harboring a bullet. Notice how

I have avoided speaking of the day
we met. I am tired of complaining
about your black gaze. You were
the dream girl become flesh.

You made a lamp out of a wine bottle
filled with lentils, split peas, millet,
for the bedside table I built of plywood
and glued cork. We were just starting out.

Cheap Sacred Wine

Pale green, pear-shaped
half-gallon wine bottle
layered with different-
colored seeds—millet,

lentils, split peas—
stopper with a socket,
lampshade antique
botanical paintings,

stood by the bed in
our brick fixer-upper
on the cork-covered
night-stand I built.

This week it turned up
on the shelf in the shed
at woods' edge. In search
of an old tool, I discovered

how the layers settled
in the jagged time
since I abandoned it.
Hers. Not mine.

To earth and wind
I returned them, seeds
unsprouted, thin scent
of wine gone broken.

To Another Single Father

My story was different from yours:
she withdrew to a nest feathered
with unread magazines, mail
cemented together by spilled tea.

I launched a personal conspiracy
to believe she was well, as if
constrained by a mask of myself,
as if the grace of our children

growing were not enough, or the safe
haven of our house in the forest.
We are not alone. It has been this way
for a long ancestry of husbands,

a continent of fathers. There is no word
for the way the water clings to leaves
when the sun reinvents itself
out of the broken storm.

The Way the Rain Works

It's the way the rain negotiates
the maze of leaves condensing
and collecting along the limbs,

down the stiff abutments of bark
or plying the slick green surface
to the leaf below, to other leaves,

anywhere but a straight path
between heaven and earth.
Where is my wife? Where are

my children tumbling down?
Water pools in the hollow places,
rain reaches the ground.

Enter the Weather

Recipe for a Heavy Heart

Pull three scallions from the rich dark soil.
Clean them. Slice them. Scatter them
in the pot where your remedy is cooking.
Add a cup of snow from your childhood,
algae from the pond, the communion
wine you didn't swallow.
Chop that honeymoon
photo, the one you forgot about,
mix it with lawn clippings, fold in
soft apples gnawed by wasps.
Offer it to the heat. How different
the ingredients taste as they blend.

Simmer to the point of tenderness,
hours, days, whatever it takes.
This is the feast you have waited for:
nothing overlooked, nothing overdone.

The Glass Heart

I went to a wedding
when the leaves fell,

her third, his second.
The wine was smooth

as old wood. I drank
two flutes, knowing

I would wake
jealous in the night,

the glass heart in the window
reflecting moonlight.

The heart is every color
and no color. It dazzles.

Turtles All the Way Down

My father married into my mother's clan
and took their blandishments
the way he drank their sherry, cautiously.
He told me he was doing research.
He said *You're one of them. I'm not.*

On the day my ninety-something Grandpa
locked himself in the bathroom,
aunts and cousins paced anxiously.
My father sat next to Grandpa's globe
in the library studying Spanish grammar.

Now the big house belongs to a cousin
with political ambitions. His children
discovered a box turtle at the wooded bend
in the drive and took it to school
in a glass terrarium, as if looking
to improve on nature, an audacity
my father never dared.
Live and let live was his motto.

One time he told the story about
the anthropologist, the shaman, and the cosmos
carried on the shoulders of giant turtles
to the brothers-in-law standing stiffly
by the sideboard, sherry glasses in hand.
He nailed the punchline
with that breathless laugh of his
like a happy dog panting for approval.

Kerosene

Straining in the breeze, a late-season
spiderweb catches the sun, the sparkling
legs of its creator rising and falling
to capture a last cold morning meal.

My son's mother's troubles are so ancient
that someday they may cease to surprise.
The dogs bark. We rush to the door.
It is nothing, I tell them. Nobody came.

Geese cross the sky in a chevron
neither south nor north, but toward
some remembered resting place.
I am always calculating what to do,

like geese, dogs, spiders, anyone.
In my dream my son and I
inhabit a cabin so volatile
that kerosene rains from the air.

Pour it on, burn it off,
bottle it, barter it,
whatever it takes
to bring this journey light.

Bright Angel

Smug in a muscle shirt, he dangles his legs
above empty space. From my side of the rail,
I watch him not fall into the abyss.
He says *You'll get over it*, brushing past
chattering girls to where Bright Angel Trail
drops below the rim. Hip-hop in ear buds,
he skitters down scree-falls, switchbacks,
vermilion tan striations of the ages.

At noon at the base of the outer canyon
in the shade of aspens where Anasazi lived,
we replenish ourselves with power bars.
Among the rocks he discovers a case knife
of turquoise and burnished wood. It gleams
in his hand. He shoulders the pack and beams.

Chamomile

Such elegant dry flowers, yellow-brown
and so delicate three years ago, when
I last tasted their good health. I hate
to let them go. I could tangle my mind

in the difficulty of knowing
the next words to tell my son, or let
the solutions arrive like cries of owls
across the distance of evening.

At that Spanish restaurant close to
his college, he said things happened
he wished he could forget. I told him
I forget a lot myself. The cleaning lady

has been in our cabinets finding salves
and remedies that are past their dates,
leaving them for us to sort out ourselves
by the stove in a plastic grocery bag.

Buck Naked at McClure's Beach

I ease between boulders
at the secluded beach's end
in search of its famous
tidal pools. A naked woman

rises in swan-like yoga
while a man equally naked
watches from the rocks and the
tide follows the sun out to sea.

Rather than choreograph some
awkward territorial dance,
I retire to the cliff's recess,
unexpectedly awed by the ocean.

The light goes golden. My love life
flows through channels unthinkable
to the innocent who once tumbled
into any arms that would have me.

In an agony of middle-aged longing
I could throw myself at the breakers,
losing control, leaping at possibilities,
emerging soaked, regretful, cold.

Instead, I clutch the wind like a cloak
and skirt waves to where starfish
huddle like mud and anemones
open their luminous hearts to the ocean.

On Two Conditions

1.

If this were normal Retinitis Pigmentosa,
when the spots coalesce you would go blind,
but in your case, only a single sector
will give way, and it will do so gradually

like a glacier, I think.

Sectoral Retinitis Pigmentosa is extremely rare.
The sector you will lose looks up and across your nose

as if for an annoying mosquito.

Back before retinal imaging
young people's sight would dim
and we would not know why.

I am shown a cloudy yellow planet
crossed by the massive river of a vein.

A patient who lost a little-used slice of vision
might not even notice.

Near a tributary, blood-red specks emerge
like tiny settlements seen from an airplane.

There is no treatment. It is hereditary.
You may tell your children what you wish.

When this condition blinds, it blinds the young.
It comes early. It is swift.
We have already skirted the accident.

2.

Cancer my first thought
when the unwelcome lumps arrive
in the palm of my hand.

                              The doctor calls it
                              Dupetryn's Syndrome

and offers a brochure showing
what to expect: first, a hand like my own
with tendons misshapen,

                              then the palm in tangles,
                              fingers turning claws.

When it gets that far, he can freeze
the sheathes with an injection
and break them in tiny pieces.

                              He tells me
                              Come back when it's time.

The brochure says this affects
older Scandinavian men.
A banner saying *Viking's Disease*
float above a dragon-headed longboat.

                      I breathe the salt air, squinting.
                      The sun dips toward the horizon.
                      My contracting hands curve to the oar.

After the Email Saying You Forgave Me

It was about the time the first
poplar leaves turn yellow.
The cottonmouth, thick as a muscular arm,
slid into the water at my feet.

The marsh burst into autumn.
Motionless in the rushes
a doe and her fawn stared
at me, necks slender, eyes intent.

Your heart would have overflowed.
The beaver arched its glossy
fantail in the far shallows.
I looked in vain for its mate as
it disappeared, wild and beautiful
in the black water, out of reach.

The Mill Dam at Bynum

In summer I wander the overgrown farm road like
    Whitman, mad and undisguised, observing how
    broad the river grows there, how poised.

Like the poet's long-limbed hymns to America the
    mill dam eases and challenges the river rushing it,
    tumbling, gushing, oozing, struggling, dribbling,
    welling, toiling, dropping. Spill, crash, sparkle,
    carry on.

In the evening, overflowing with secret love, I dangle
    my feet above the receding spillway and listen:
    ripples. The moon's reflection rides them like a
    blessing.

Don't Say There Is Pure Consciousness

or that it inhabits everything
or that if you lived this your troubles
would dissolve and be as nothing,
not even if the life-changing vision of Ezekiel
reveals to you the inner workings of creation,
its burning wheels within wheels.

Once my teacher told me
You must drown the mind.
Another time he said
Don't try so hard
and when I last saw him,
Treat yourself with kindness.

If you experience pure consciousness
for even a flash, you might find yourself
dancing around that vision for years,
for a lifetime, coaxing it to return
to the nest you have woven for it
out of the little branches inside your heart.

The Things I Do When I Am Alone

I learned from
you, to sit

with the falling
leaves, slice

a pear into sections
eat it slowly

as if solitude
were that sweet

and still

Enter the Weather

Stainless sky.
A car starts. The wind
rustles every leaf
in every tree.
The kitchen garden shivers:
mint, parsley, peppers
a forest of silent motion.
Close by
a wren is calling.

We are of animals
and angels. The wind
rises like an ocean.
The weather of our lives
begins to turn.

Birthday Ending in Zero

No rain for days, and on the pollen-dusted porch
a vase of flowers arrived from nowhere:

yellow roses, lilies, carnations, tulips with orange tips
and stems of electric-blue buds like paper lanterns.

We were happy in that second Covid spring, gathering
our loved ones on Zoom, cooking fish with asparagus,

ate our apple pie and still it didn't rain. In the pollen
on the back deck, small animals left yellow footprints.

That week, after so long alone, you let go
into the space we had begun to share.

You stood the flowers on the kitchen table
surrounded with gifts and letters from my friends.

Our hearts opened like small animals looking around.
We slept skin to skin, your presence rippling like a lake.

That week the huge heads of the roses unfolded in radi-
ance even as the water started to cloud.

even as carnations drooped and tulip petals dropped.
When the rain began I found a ravine where no one goes

and under the trees, scattered the globes of the roses,
tulips with their falling petals, lilies and lanterns.

Wild Strawberries

Though I seldom find them now, I am sure
they will be there when I need them, small
and bright and immensely sweet, in the orchard
where my brothers and I learned to drive

the jeep with the shuddering gearbox, or on
the slope behind the stadium, *Brown-Eyed Girl*
and *Night Moves* filling the airwaves with longing
when I loved an urbane strawberry blonde

in a sweet passion in a gilded-age house
but she was never the kind to climb with me
skirting poison ivy by the stadium's steel underside
to taste the wild berries, and to this day

I fail to understand how I found
the berries, or her, or anything in this life.

Just last night I cut a pulpy fruit, hollow
and white inside. I cut several of them, strawberries
for a new millennium, firm against my thumb,
their bruised leaves wet and scented,

to make strawberry shortcake with biscuits
and cream. It is the strawberries that matter.
I want to give my children something fresh
and fine, with a flavor to believe in.

A Dream Nobody Chose

Before the Bus Stops

You will see a man
tearing corrugated iron,
you will see children
you wish you had not seen,
you will see colorful flags
trampled in mud.

This travel is harder
than you imagined.
Behind your shoulder
sunlight slices the window.

Before the bus stops, ask
the man with the bad back
about the news from home.
Maybe he will say *It is fine,*
maybe *There is no home.*

Offer to share your dinner.
Ask about the people
he left behind.
Maybe you remind him
of somebody he knows.
You and he are traveling
in a dream nobody chose.

Signature of Extinction

Varengeville-sur-mer,
Normandie

A thin black seam in the strata
ten feet above the beach, the signature
of the Chicxulub meteor half a world
and sixty-five million years away.

The explosion welled
through the fleeing, expanding air.
Ash rained on the ocean. Pulverized
iridium and sandstone

drifted down with carcasses
of ichthyosaurs, plesiosaurs, pterosaurs.
Our tiny mammal ancestors fled
from what was tumbling from the sky.

Glaciers melt, rivers dry.
Insect populations crash,
all the biggest animals quickly gone,
crocodiles hunkered in cold burrows.

Ferns returned first
to the scarred continents,
then trees, a few small birds,
mammals, wind in branches.

Silt accumulated, layer upon layer.
Europe lifted from the shallow sea
whose waves beat the cliff base back
to expose the extinction signature.

In our own time the bees disappear,
the salamanders and songbirds. Insects
no longer smack against our windshields
in this land we are leaving.

Some say humans are leaving their mark
on every genome, every natural resource.
Anthropocene, the era of humans—
call it an extinction event, a new black line

to decorate the cliffs of sixty million years
from now, plastic and depleted uranium
our signature, spent glitter and asphalt
compressed into a narrow slice of rock.

Last Elm in Addison County

Let's walk out to the big elm, my mother would say
on a summer evening, sun low across the valley.
Half a mile back in the field it raised
the elegant lily of its branches against the ridge

of the Green Mountains. It was our landmark
in all seasons. It tethered us to our new home.
We would stroll to a pasture where curious Holsteins
poked their muzzles through the fence, and took alfalfa

from our outstretched hands. Crickets surrounded us
with their buzz. At the end of the rutted farm road,
we waded through a sea of grass to the base of the tree.
This was the spot to see the last of the light

playing across the bottomland corn crops.
Shadows climbed the skirts of the mountains,
one rocky ridge after another, even to the edge
of our own farm, even where we stood.

Uncle Jack's Last Invention

From his sunlit bed the day after his fall
he tells me about the Able Mouse he's created
for arthritic hands. His prototype can sense
a single pixel, but the patent process is slow.

I hold his hand and we talk about the pleasure
he took in the letters from my mother so long ago.
He is 96, and says he has one, maybe two more years
of the clarity he needs to complete the Mouse

or maybe it's gone already. He explains
how the software responds to movement,
the way a leg lifts and a foot sets down.

My Father Walks Out of the World Trade Center

After the millennium,
after my mother passed away,
after the towers fell,
he dreamed he was navigating slowly
down the crowded stairwell
into the noise, the smell, the smoke,
an old man unsure of his footing,
working his way back down
to the twentieth century,
where everything he loved was new,
where his wife sang in the garden.

The Body's Small Purposes

His lungs like exhausted fishermen
drew in their glittering catch
of oxygen and his heart
called to the receding tides of the blood.
His bony fingers curled around mine.
I read from Mary Oliver

how the soul may be hard, necessary,
yet almost nothing, how we all know
the sand is golden under the cold waves
though our hands can never touch it.

The hearing goes last, the doctor said.

There are no words for this communion,
this hope that his eyes, turned from
the sunny branches outside, could summon
a vision of loved ones long gone,
wife of fifty years, sister dead in childbirth,
souls knowing already this passage
and awaiting him in whatever form of glory
the living can conjure: my brothers, me,
our children, all the others
still casting the nets of our breath,
still sifting the golden sands.

Once in his search for love after my mother died
he told me it never ends. But it does.
On a broken day the breath stops
and the cells gently fall asleep
and the soul, perhaps puzzled
by this coming to rest
of all the body's small purposes
rises and looks on the silence.

Satchel Recedes in the Trees

At the fringe of the lopped and leveled
countryside where boxy houses rise
we would wander down gullies under oaks
as the evening deepened.

I kept track of him by the glow
of his yellow coat as he splashed
the marsh's edge with ungainly paws.
He kept track of me by my scent.

I wanted to walk out of myself
into a darkness thick with early stars.
Satchel took us the other way,
toward dinner and home.

Tonight the woods seem transparent,
like a dream of the half-erased path
where we would wander, dry leaves
underfoot, crescent moon in the trees.

Even at the end, Satchel used his nose
to keep us on the path. That was his job,
to lead me home, his eyes filled
with a fading light I can still discern.

The Last Purple Blossoms

Still the cicadas, fall coming,
days shorter and cool. The sun
hangs in branches thick with green,
tomatoes not quite ripening, yellow
leaves on the geranium, the last
purple blossoms of petunia.
My ex-wife has texted me
a long enumeration
of how I have failed my children
and will likely fail my grandchild.

Every day the insistent call
of the messages rings more distant.
Love's threads will pull me through.

Shimmy and Clatter

Sycamore leaves lie brown on my deck.
On the trees they rustle
as if nothing happens much
except the wind.

I have listened to this music all my life.

This morning I read Rilke and Rimbaud.
The leaves shimmy and clatter.
I was a teacher once. I had ambitions.

In the silence
the sound of a distant hammer.

True singing
is a gust in the god, a wind.
Rilke's sentences rise like angels.

Rimbaud's swirl in the falling leaves:
The dream is growing cold.

I have sung these songs
since I was a child.
The wind rises,
the wind rushes and whispers.

Let Us All Be Happy

the train glides through spring green
whistle moaning at every crossing
every seat taken   families eating sandwiches
two men behind me swapping recipes

down the aisle comes the conductor
a tall woman   dark curls
white railroad blouse   pushing
a waist-high transparent trash sack

half filled   with plastic drink cups
hamburger boxes   water bottles
ladies and gentlemen she says
her reassuring voice filling the car

do you have any trash   the woman
on her way to relatives in Charlotte
reaches across me   to drop in
what is left of her lunch

the conductor moves past a trembling lady
with thin grey hair   *do you have any trash*
moves past her younger companion
past the men trading recipes

ladies and gentlemen says the conductor
let us all be happy   ladies and gentlemen
as we slowly take our leave of this world
so random   and so transient   let us all be happy

Acknowledgements

My fellow Black Socks Poets—Grey Brown, Janis Harrington, Maura High, Paul Jones, Debra Kaufman, Florence Nash, Gary Phillips, and Liza Wolff-Francis—deserve special thanks for their careful readings and occasionally humbling critiques, always in the service of enabling the poetry to shine. Debra, Jan, and Paul worked through the entire manuscript at various phases, helping immensely with the overall conception and structure, as did my lifelong poet friends, Chapman Hood Frazier and Don Wildman. Eric Sundquist also provided welcome feedback. Winston Fuller launched me on this poetic voyage many years ago, well-provisioned with ideas, technique, and spirit, and William Harmon taught me to do what comes naturally, no matter what anybody thinks.

I would particularly like to express my gratitude to Judith Valerie, my partner of fourteen years, whose unwavering support is as priceless as her keen poetic ear, and my sons Ethan and Luke, whose own journeys intertwine with mine throughout these pages.

Many thanks to the editors of the following publications in which versions of these poems first appeared:

And Love . . .: The Things I Do When I Am Alone
Cairn: Kerosene
Carolina Quarterly: The Insulating Properties of
    Trees
Hampden-Sydney Review: The Huge House Among
    Trees
Hermit Feathers Review: Betty Helps Out
Indelible: A Man Like You Deserves French Fries
Kakalak: City of Thorns, Wild Strawberries
One: Any Snake Bears Watching
Pinesong: Bring Me Back the Change, Last Elm in
    Addison County, My Father Walks Out of the
    World Trade Center
Poetry in Plain Sight: Enter the Weather
Red Fez: We Lived on the Edge of Calamity
Running With Water: Birthday Ending in Zero
StorySouth: Every Field of Paradise
The Orchards Poetry Journal: The Glass Heart
The Sun: After the Email Saying You Forgave Me,
    The Body's Small Purposes, Nor Do They Talk
Tar River Poetry: The Cormorants Arrive, Early
    Morning Light, The Mill Dam at Bynum
Third Wednesday: Before the Bus Stops
Triggerfish Critical Review: Green Patchwork of
    Morning, The Small Kitchen Appliances Aisle,
    What Becomes of the Strawberries, When I Hitch-
    hiked to Big Sur
Verse Virtual: How We Lost the Beehives

The following poems appeared in *The Way the Rain
    Works* (Greensboro, NC: Sable Books, 2015):
    Buck Naked at McClure's Beach, Chamomile,
    Every Field of Paradise, First Light, The Insulating
    Properties of Trees, Snow Falling Silently, Still Life
    with Shovel, Still Life with Chainsaw, The Things
    I Do When I Am Alone, The Way the Rain Works,
    When the Sun Reinvents Itself

About the Author

 After a childhood in Connecticut and Vermont, Ralph Earle has lived in the North Carolina Triangle since 1977. He holds a Ph.D. in English from UNC-Chapel Hill, where he taught poetry before founding a bookstore, then pursuing a career in technical communications. Currently, he designs websites for poets and other creative people. His poems have appeared in over 30 publications, and his collection *The Way the Rain Works* won the 2015 Sable Books Chapbook Award. He co-manages a monthly poetry reading in Chapel Hill and has twice been nominated for a Pushcart Prize.